P9-CQG-938

ECOSYSTEMS

Life in a
Rain Forest

Stuart P. Levine

KIDHAVEN
PRESS™

THOMSON

GALE

San Diego • Detroit • New York • San Francisco • Cleveland
New Haven, Conn. • Waterville, Maine • London • Munich

LIBRARY OF CONGRESS CATALOGING-IN-PUBLICATION DATA

Levine, Stuart P.
  Life in a rain forest / by Stuart P. Levine.
    v. cm. — (The ecosystems library)
Includes bibliographical references and index.
Contents: What is a rain forest? — The top layers of the rain forest — The bottom
layers of the rain forest — The endangered rain forest.
  ISBN 0-7377-1533-2 (hardback : alk. paper)
  1. Rain forest ecology—Juvenile literature. [1. Rain forest ecology. 2. Ecology.]
I. Title. II. Series.
  QH541.5.R27L477 2003
  577.34—dc21
                            2002154429

Printed in China

Contents

Chapter 1

What Is a Rain Forest?

Although most forests are filled with wildlife, such as tall trees, beautiful flowers, and a wide assortment of animals, there is one type of forest that has more life in it than any other. It is called the rain forest. These lush, tropical forests are packed with millions of different types of trees and plants, some of which grow more than two hundred feet tall. There are countless species of birds, mammals, reptiles, and insects that live amongst all the dense foliage. Millions of years ago, rain forests covered most of the earth's surface. Today they cover only between 5 and 7 percent. As small a part of the world as rain forests have become, they are still home to more than half of all life on the planet.

Where in the World?

With less than 3 million square miles of rain forest left in the world, scientists have spent a lot of time studying the ones that remain. More than half of the world's tropical rain forests can be found in South America along the Amazon River. While the Amazon and its surrounding rain forests run through a number of countries, most of the Amazon lies within the borders of Brazil. The next-largest area of rain forest is located

Sunbeams pierce the treetops of a misty rain forest. Rain forests contain more than half of all life on Earth.

on the other side of the world. In Southeast Asia, a large chain of rain forests runs through Indonesia, Malaysia, New Guinea, and the Philippines. These forests cover an area of approximately 500,000 square miles. The third-largest pocket of rain forest is only slightly smaller, at 400,000 square miles. It runs along the Congo River basin in central and western Africa. As far apart as these three areas are, they have one thing in common: They all lie on or near the equator. This is no coincidence. The equator is the warmest part of the earth, and warmth is one of the elements that makes a forest a rain forest.

Constant Warmth and Moisture

For an area to be called a tropical rain forest, it needs constant warmth. The farther a region is from the equator, the more temperatures vary throughout the

Dense clouds descend on a rain forest and act like a greenhouse over the tropical canyon.

year. Winters are very cold, and summers are very hot. Since the equator is about the same distance from the sun all year long, the temperature there stays the same all the time. Most tropical rain forests are between seventy and eighty degrees every day of the year.

The other important element in a rain forest is rain. In some parts of the world, it hardly ever rains. In most places, it just rains once in a while. In the rain forest it rains every single day. Most rain forests receive anywhere from one hundred to four hundred inches of rain each year. That is nearly ten times the amount of rain that falls in the United States each year and up to forty times as much rain as most deserts receive.

All of this moisture and heat creates a place that feels a lot like a greenhouse. Just like in a greenhouse, the plants thrive and grow all year long.

Food for the Forest

Other types of forests store a lot of rich nutrients in their soil, but the rain forest does not. Instead of getting

nutrients from deep in the soil, trees use the constant supply of leaf litter on the ground. Leaf litter is a combination of dead leaves, tree branches, fallen fruit, and animal droppings. These things decompose, or fall apart, very quickly in the rain forest. As the rain pours down each day, the nutrients from all the leaf litter wash into the ground. The shallow tree roots soak up the nutrients right away and use the energy to help grow new leaves, flowers, and fruits.

All of this new life budding on the trees serves as food for a host of different animals. Many bees live on the nectar in the brightly colored flowers. Parrots and monkeys feed on the tasty fruit. Even the leaves make a crunchy meal for treetop iguanas. When these ani-

An iguana balances atop a tree stump. Iguanas depend on the nutrient-rich leaves that grow in the rain forest.

A dark thundercloud looms over a mountainside. Daily storms help recycle important nutrients.

mals drop part of their meal, or leave behind droppings of their own, they are recycling their leftovers to the forest floor, where it can be used again.

The Daily Storm

This continuous recycling of energy and living matter in the rain forest is made possible by the constant heat and rain. Each day, after the rain has fallen, the heat causes the standing water to turn to mist. The humid air rises, carrying all that moisture back up to the clouds. The higher it goes, the cooler the air becomes. When it gets so high and so cool that the mist starts turning back into drops of water, a cloud is formed. The sky begins to darken and, quietly at first, thunder begins to roll in. When the cloud gets big enough and heavy enough, the thunder becomes much louder. Just moments after the first drops of water can be heard splashing off the leaves of the tallest trees, the clouds burst open. They dump all the water they have been collecting back down on the forest. The rain is very loud and can last for several hours. Coming down in great storming sheets, it drowns out nearly all other sounds and sights in the rain forest. This daily flooding washes all of the nutrients from the leaf litter back into the soil, and the cycle begins again.

A World on Its Own

The rain forest is nearly a closed system in nature. This means it can survive on its own without much influence from outside **ecosystems**. It generates its own climate, food sources, plants, animals, and even oxygen. The rain forest is able to sustain itself so neatly because of the incredible variety that exists there. Scientists estimate that at least 30 million species of plants and animals live in the rain forest, making it the most diverse ecosystem on Earth. Where all of this life exists, and how it all fits together, is one of the most fascinating stories in nature.

Layers of a Rain Forest

Emergent Layer
This level contains only the highest tree tops, some as high as 200 feet. Emergent trees are home to predators such as hawks and eagles.

Canopy
Just below the tallest emergent trees, this level contains thousands of plant and animal species. This level also provides cover for the lower levels of the rain forest.

Forest Floor
Although very little light or water reaches this level, the forest floor provides important nutrients for the trees above. Giant flowers, rodents, and large predators live here.

Understory
This area receives very little sunlight and is home to moss, algae, and vines. A variety of bugs and other small animals live here.

The Layers of the Rain Forest

This amazing diversity of life is packed into every square inch of the ecosystem. Most of the plants and animals are adapted to live in one of four levels of the rain forest. The bottom layers, which contain the **understory** and **forest floor**, are typically dark and the things that live there can survive without much light. The upper layers, including the **canopy** and **emergent layer**, are drenched in light. These upper layers contain most of the life in the rain forest.

Chapter 2

The Top of the Rain Forest

The very top of the rain forest is called the emergent layer. It is made up of the very tallest trees. These trees can reach heights of over two hundred feet, which is as high as some of the tallest buildings in a city. The emergent trees look like giant green umbrellas that have popped open above the roof, or canopy, of the rain forest. Most of the trees at this level are called **dipterocarps**.

Dipterocarps, or tropical hardwoods, grow very straight and tall, with hardly any branches or leaves at their lower levels. Their strong trunks work for many years to raise the crown of the tree up toward the sky. In fact, some dipterocarps, such as the Mengaris tree of Malaysia, do not reach maturity and begin producing fruit until they are sixty years old.

These trees work so hard to reach these heights because they need the sunlight to live. Sunlight is a precious commodity in the rain forest; it provides one of the most important ingredients in the diet of a plant. Most plants get their nutrients through a pro-

A hardwood tree towers above the canopy of the rain forest.

cess known as **photosynthesis**. This is a chemical reaction that takes place in the plant and allows it to convert sunlight into energy. The more sunlight a plant can absorb, the more food, or energy, it can produce for itself. Once a tree has succeeded in reaching the emergent layer, it will have all the sunlight it needs.

Is Anyone Home?

Although there may be an ample supply of sunlight in the emergent layer, there is very little protection from the elements. Emergent trees are often spread out from one another across great distances. The crown of each dipterocarp is like an island in the sky. The direct heat, rain, and strong wind at these heights make it difficult for most animals to survive. With so few animals living at this layer, a tree cannot depend on animals to spread its seeds. Instead, emergent trees rely on the wind. Unlike other rainforest trees, dipterocarps have light, fluffy seeds, with leafy "wings" attached to them. When these seeds come loose from the tree, they glide, or "helicopter," away in the wind to plant themselves off at great distances.

A few animals, however, do live in the emergent layer. Although the unprotected crowns of these trees pose a threat to some animals, they provide perfect vantage points for the aerial hunters of the rain forest to look for their next meal. Several **raptors**, or birds of prey, live up in these trees. Hawks and eagles, for example, will take advantage of the great view to easily spot a tasty morsel. With a highly developed sense of sight, they can pick out and grab something as small as a mouse scurrying through the thick branches of the canopy below. Some raptors, however, such as the harpy eagle of South America, go after much larger prey. One of the largest birds of prey in the world, the harpy eagle will catch and eat monkeys and even the occasional sloth. The animals in the canopy below must always remain alert if they hope to survive.

The Canopy

Only a small amount of sunlight and rain is blocked by the sparse emergent trees. So, 90 percent of these life-giving elements reach the plants and animals of the canopy, where trees grow from 60 to 120 feet tall. However, unlike the emergent layer, the canopy is a thick tangle of branches, leaves, and vines. It provides great shelter from the elements and from many **predators**. This so-called roof of the rain forest is where most of the plant and animal life can be found.

Trees such as the white lauan make a perfect home for a host of birds, mammals, insects, reptiles, and even other plants. There are monkeys, such as the capuchin, that live in large family groups as well as solitary animals like the coendou, or prehensile-tailed porcupine, that like to live by themselves. Many species of colorful parrots can be seen flying and

The South American harpy eagle (inset) nests in the tallest emergent trees of the rain forest, where it scouts the canopy for prey (above).

A venomous parrot snake prepares to strike. Snakes and lizards are common rain-forest animals.

climbing along the treetop highways in search of tasty fruit. Snakes and lizards live up here as well, waiting to make a meal out of an unsuspecting rodent, bird, or insect. These predators do not have it easy, though. Many insects have amazing **camouflage** to help them blend into their surroundings. The katydid, for example, has large green wings that make it look just like a leaf. Unless it moves, it is nearly impossible to spot.

Air Plants

Giant trees and animals are not the only things that find a home at this layer. There are also plants called **epiphytes** that live on the surface of the trees instead of in the soil. An orchid, for example, is a type of epiphyte. The tall trees of the canopy provide epiphytes access to the sunlight and rain near the forest roof. They are able to gather moisture right out of the air. Their long roots, which spread along the branches of their host tree, will gather any nutrients nearby. Some

Epiphytes cover a fallen tree, providing a safe haven for camouflaged insects (inset).

of these nutrients come in the form of animal droppings or dead leaves that get caught in the treetops. Even the remains of old epiphytes serve as a source of nutrition. As the old epiphytes die, they decompose in the canopy and form what is called **crown humus**. This material provides a bed upon which new epiphytes can grow.

The vibrant tank bromeliad collects rainwater with its cuplike leaves.

A juvenile stick insect clings to a leaf shortly after hatching. Insects are an important part of rain-forest ecology.

Even though these epiphytes grow on the trees, they usually do not hurt their hosts. Most epiphytes have what is called a **symbiotic** relationship with the rest of the forest life around them. In other words, they help each other out. The epiphytes use the height of the tree to reach the sun and water they need, but the plants in turn provide shelter and nutrients for many occupants of the canopy. The tank bromeliad, for example, is an epiphyte whose flower is shaped like an upright cup. It collects water and provides a place for certain species of frogs and insects to lay their eggs.

Working Together

All things in nature are connected in one way or another, but this connection is rarely clearer than in the canopy of a rain forest. For example, several types of biting ants live off the sap inside of trees. These ants live in the bark of the tree, and when animals come to the tree to strip off new leaves or flowers, the ants come out in force and bite them until they leave. The tree provides sap for the ants, and the ants provide protection for the tree.

However, trees do need some animals to feed off them in order to survive. In fact, most species of canopy trees depend on the local animals for spreading seeds and **pollination**. Seeds often grow inside the tree's fruit. The fruit attracts a number of different animals, such as monkeys, birds, and fruit bats. These animals will eat the fruit and seeds and, unknowingly, deposit them through their droppings somewhere else in the forest. Wherever a seed falls, there is the potential for a new tree to grow and, someday, provide a home and food for many other canopy dwellers. Without all of these important players, the canopy could never survive.

Chapter 3

The Bottom of the Rain Forest

Very little light or rain reaches the bottom layers of the rain forest. Most of these life-giving elements are blocked by the dense canopy overhead. In the understory layer, the trees are only between ten and twenty feet tall. These trees grow slowly and wait patiently for their chance to reach new heights. The plants and animals that live in this layer are well adapted for life in the dark. For example, understory trees have large leaves to give them a better chance of catching whatever sun and water make it to their level. However, with all this darkness, water that collects does not easily evaporate. Water and darkness is the perfect formula for moss and algae, which can grow rapidly across a plant and damage or even kill it. To combat this, large leaves often have drip spouts built into them. This allows excess water to run off the leaves and prevents too much moss and algae from growing.

A Vine to Swing From

Most of what can be found at this layer are tree trunks and vines that are climbing their way up toward the canopy. Similar to epiphytes, vines, or "climbers," are a group of plants that live on other, larger plants. Climbers, however, have their roots firmly planted in the ground and grow up the trunks of the trees. Some vines are soft, and others, such as the liana, have a stiff, woody exterior. These climbers will latch onto tree trunks using a variety of different thorns, hooks, and spines. The most successful vines will climb their way right out of the understory and into the canopy, There, they will flourish into a leafy network of stems that crisscross the entire roof of the rain forest.

Animals in the Understory

The lower layers are not as thick with plants as the upper layers, and a few creatures take full advantage of all this space. Some birds, such as the antshrike and the hummingbird, make nests in the understory trees, where they can raise their young away from the hungry talons of hawks and eagles. A number of termite species make their nests on the sides of the thick trunks.

The nests are made from chewed wood and termite saliva, which is nearly as hard as concrete. These nests provide great protection from hungry **insectivores**. However, the tamandua, or lesser anteater, has very

Thick, woody vines extend across the rain-forest floor.

sharp, powerful claws. It knows that termites build their nests here, and it spends hours looking for them. Once located, the tamandua will tear open the nest and get at the tasty termites inside.

Termites use their powerful jaws (inset) to build nests out of chewed wood and saliva.

The Forest Floor

The lowest layer of the rain forest is the forest floor. Like the basement of a building, this layer is often very dark and silent. Only 10 percent of the rain that falls each day reaches this layer and, in some places, less than 1 percent of the sunlight. As a result, there is less activity here than in the upper layers or even in the understory. The forest floor, however, does have an important role to play.

Since the nutrients are all needed way up above, the bases of the trees on the forest floor have to be good at gathering this food and sending it up. Most of these trees have a highly developed root system designed for this purpose. However, since the nutrients are all near the surface of the soil, the roots only go down a few feet into the ground. This presents a small problem. In most forests, deep roots are what anchor the trees into the ground, offering them support and stability.

One quick glance at the bases of the trees explains how the rain forest handles this challenge. Many of the taller trees, which need the most support, have what are called buttress roots. Ordinary roots come out of the bottom of the tree and go straight into the ground. They are invisible from above the ground. Buttress roots, however, come right out of the tree's trunk, above the ground, and burrow down into the soil. These powerful roots branch out from as high as ten feet up the trunk. Acting like training wheels on a bicycle, these buttress roots provide the support the tree needs to stand up at such great heights.

Life on the Forest Floor

Some plants and animals do live on the forest floor. Fungi are a type of plant that can exist without light. Instead of getting their energy from the sun, they collect it from other sources, such as decaying matter. Mushrooms are a type of fungus. Thousands of different kinds of fungi grow on the forest floor. Many of them, such as the red fungus of South America, look like flowers blooming on fallen logs. The fungus is an extremely important part of the rain-forest ecosystem because it helps to decompose rotting material. It converts all these materials into a usable form, making the forest floor into a giant pantry of nutrients for the plants and animals that need them. There are also many types of insects, such as termites and ants, that will spend their time breaking down the materials they find on the ground.

Giant Flowers and Rodents

Besides fungi and insects, there are a few other ground dwellers in the forest. A variety of low-light plants, such as ferns, can be seen sprawling across the ground. One unusual plant on the forest floor is the giant rafflesia. Growing in the rain forests of Asia, the rafflesia's flower is the largest in the world. It can grow to be three feet from end to end and can weigh up to twenty-five pounds.

One animal that makes its home on the floor of the South American rain forest is the agouti. The agouti is a large rodent that eats fruits, leaves, flowers,

Tiny, flowerlike mushrooms sprout from a rotting log on the forest floor.

and nuts. It has a brownish red coat, a tiny stub of a tail, and, like most rodents, very powerful teeth. The agouti's hind legs are much longer than its front legs, which gives it an amazing jumping ability. It can jump six feet straight up in the air. This helps it to avoid the many predators that might want to make a meal out of it. One of those predators, the jaguar, lives on the floor of the forest as well. The jaguar will often sleep in a tree a few feet above the ground and then come

Rain-Forest Predators

Turkey Vulture
Brazil

**Emerald
Tree Boa**
Amazon
River Basin

**Hunting
Spider**
Costa Rica

Jaguar
Amazon
River Basin

Weaver Ants
Malaysia

The forest floor is home to many species of insects such as this Malaysian long-horned beetle.

down to hunt at night. Its excellent night vision, combined with great strength and agility, make it one of the most dangerous hunters in the South American rain forest.

Whether drenched in light or masked beneath a veil of darkness, each layer has its own important part to play in the rain-forest ecosystem as a whole. As different as they all may be, they do have one thing in common: All of the plants and animals of the rain forest are currently fighting a battle for their survival.

Chapter 4

The Endangered Rain Forest

Rain forests all over the world are disappearing at an alarming rate. In the twentieth century alone, over half of the world's rain forests were leveled.

When a stretch of rain forest disappears, all the rich variety of plant and animal life that lived there is lost as well. That variety includes millions of species of plants and animals. Scientists estimate that anywhere from 5 million to 25 million different types of plants and animals live in the rain-forest canopy alone. This level of diversity is found nowhere else in the world. For example, studies have shown that one single rain-forest tree in Brazil can house more unique species of ants than all of the British Isles.

The Value of the Land

People cut down trees in the rain forest for a number of different reasons. One of the main reasons is the need for timber. Tropical hardwoods, or dipterocarps, are very large and very strong. Each felled tree represents a large quantity of valuable lumber that is

An eroded hillside is all that remains of a cleared rain forest.

resistant to wear, rot, and even insects. The timber industry is most active in the rain forests of Southeast Asia. In Thailand, for example, about 80 percent of the rain forests have been cleared. Trees from these forests have been turned into lumber.

The other primary use for rain-forest land is agriculture. As human populations grow, more land is cleared to grow food or raise livestock. Because the soil in a rain forest is not very rich, once the trees and leaf litter are removed, crops do not grow there for very long. After just a few years, the farmers must abandon the land and go in search of new rain forest to clear. In this way, millions of acres of rain forest are cleared every year to be used for cattle ranching or farming. This problem is most common in Central America, where more than two-thirds of the rain forests have been cleared by ranchers.

More than Just a Tree

When an area of rain forest is cut down, animals also suffer. Without the trees that provide food and shelter, the animals that live there cannot survive. The wooly spider monkey of Brazil, for example, lives almost exclusively on leaves found in the rain forest. Ninety-five percent of its habitat, and its source of food, has disappeared. As a result, it is now the rarest of the South American primates. In the 1970s, scientists realized that only three thousand of them were left in the world. Today, there are only seven hundred.

Native Peoples

Plants and animals are not the only ones that live in the rain forest. Even today, some tribes of **indigenous**, or native, people still live there. As the rain forests are cut down and modern society enters their world, these people's lives and cultures are changed forever. Currently, about 140 million indigenous people live in rain forests. They come from about one thousand different cultures. Each year some of these cultures disappear. Many of their people die from diseases accidentally introduced by Westerners.

Every year thousands of young people from these tribes leave behind their traditional ways and move to

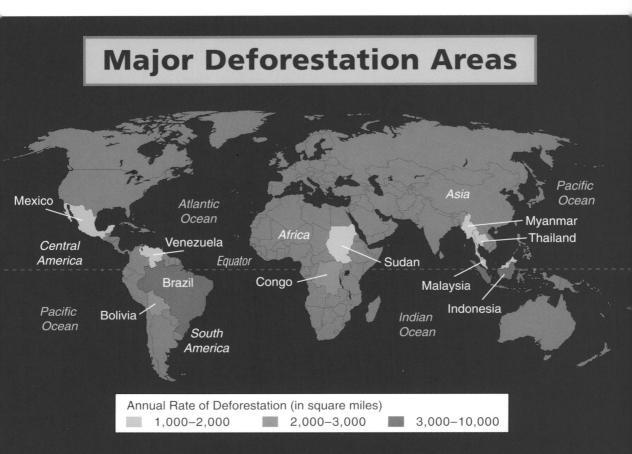

Major Deforestation Areas

Mexico

Atlantic
Ocean

Asia

Pacific
Ocean

Central
America

Venezuela

Africa

Myanmar
Thailand

Equator

Sudan

Pacific
Ocean

Brazil

Congo

Malaysia

Bolivia

Indonesia

South
America

Indian
Ocean

Annual Rate of Deforestation (in square miles)
1,000–2,000   2,000–3,000   3,000–10,000

A Yanomami boy uses a mirror to paint his face. Many indigenous cultures face extinction due to loss of the rain forest.

cities to seek education and wealth. For the individual, this may not be a bad thing, but for his or her culture, it means **extinction**. For example, the Yanomami people of Brazil numbered about 8 million before Western society entered their world. Today, just a few decades later, there are only two hundred thousand Yanomami left.

Rain-Forest Resources

It is not just the local people of the rain forest who are affected by the loss of habitat. The rain forest provides humans all over the world with a large number of valuable resources. Over three thousand fruits and nuts come from the rain forest. Things like bananas, oranges, pineapples, mangos, coffee, pepper, chocolate, cinnamon, and vanilla were all discovered in the rain forest. Most of the rubber used today comes from the rubber trees of South America.

As people discover how dangerous chemical pesticides are to the environment, scientists turn to the rain forest for more natural alternatives. Many trees have natural chemicals that can ward off certain insects. Many of these chemicals are being studied for use in large-scale pest control.

One of the most important things to have come out of the rain forest is medicine. A plant called the rosy periwinkle, for example, was used to develop a drug to treat leukemia, a form of cancer that attacks the blood.

Medicinal plants such as the rosy periwinkle (inset) and the yage vine are used to treat disease.

Since the introduction of this medicine, leukemia patients now have a 90 percent chance of making a full recovery. Currently, 25 percent of all medicines used in the world came from rain-forest plants.

So far, scientists have studied less than 1 percent of rain-forest plant species. This means there may be an endless number of new foods out there or a cure for almost any disease. Scientists may never get the chance to discover them though, as many of these plants become extinct before they are ever discovered.

Does the Earth Need the Rain Forest?

Not only does the rain forest hold a lot of value for the human species, but it serves a global purpose as well. The small belt of rain forest, which stretches across the equator, plays a large part in controlling the environment and weather of the planet. Sometimes referred to as "the lungs of the earth," rain-forest trees recycle the atmosphere and, through photosynthesis, produce vast quantities of oxygen.

Many nature organizations, governments, and even individual people are working hard to find ways to save the rain forest. The key to protecting this habitat is education. The more people know about how important the rain forest is to their everyday life and to that of the earth itself, the greater the chance this unique ecosystem and all of its diverse inhabitants will remain a part of the world.

Glossary

camouflage: Coloration that helps an animal blend into its surroundings.

canopy: The layer of the rain forest that contains the majority of plant and animal life.

crown humus: Nutrient-rich debris that gets trapped in the branches of trees.

dipterocarps: Very tall rain-forest trees, also known as tropical hardwoods.

ecosystem: The connected network of plants, animals, and weather systems that make up a specific pocket of nature.

emergent layer: The layer of the rain forest that contains the tallest tree tops.

epiphyte: A type of plant that lives off the branches of other trees instead of in the soil.

extinct: A species that has completely vanished from the earth.

forest floor: The ground and underbrush of the rain forest.

indigenous: Native to a particular area.

insectivore: An animal that eats insects.

photosynthesis: A chemical process used by plants to convert sunlight and carbon dioxide into energy.

pollination: A step in the reproductive process of plants that results in the creation of a seed.

predator: An animal that hunts other animals for food.

raptor: A type of bird that hunts other animals for food.

symbiotic: When two plant or animal species have a relationship that is beneficial to both.

understory: The layer of the rainforest that contains small trees and animals that live on them.

For Further Exploration

Books

Toni Albert, *The Remarkable Rainforest: An Active-Learning Book for Kids.* Mechanicsburg, PA: Trickle Creek Books, 1996. An interactive book that teaches about rain-forest ecology, plants, and animals through a variety of fun activities and projects.

Tim Knight, *Journey into the Rainforest.* New York: Oxford University Press, 2001. This book is set up as a travel guide to the rain forest. It describes what you would need if you went there and some of the amazing things you would see. It is filled with many beautiful pictures and illustrations.

Scott Lewis, *The Rainforest Book.* New York: Berkley Book, 1990. This book describes the many fascinating parts of the rain forest and gives suggestions for ways to help protect it.

Will Osborne and Mary Pope Osborne, *Magic Tree House Research Guide: Rainforests.* New York: Random House, 2001. The authors provide descriptions of many different plant and animal species that live in the rain forest.

Websites

Rainforest Action Network (www.RAN.org). The Rainforest Action Network is dedicated to education about and protection of rain-forest habitats and the people who live in and around them. Its website is full of interesting, user-friendly information and has some great children's interactive learning areas.

Rainforest Links (www.rain-tree.com). This site offers links to a large number of nonprofit organizations that work to protect the world's rain forests. Many different types of organizations are represented on this page.

The Rainforest Site (www.therainforestsite.com). The Rainforest Site provides a wealth of information about rain forests around the world. Its focus is on ways to help protect rain forests and it even has a free donation feature that uses advertising sponsors' funds to make donations to rain forests whenever you click on the designated "donate" button.

Index

lizards, 18
lumber, 33–34
"lungs of the earth," 38

Malaysia, 13
medicines, 37–38
mice, 16
monkeys, 8, 16, 34
moss, 24
mushrooms, 28

native peoples, 35–36
New Guinea, 6
nutrients
  animal droppings as,
    8–9
  in canopy layer, 20
  on forest floor, 27, 28
  leaf litter as, 8, 10
  photosynthesis and,
    14–15

orchids, 18

parrots, 8, 16, 18
Philippines, 6
photosynthesis, 14–15
plants
  air, 18–21
  in canopy layer, 18–21,
    24, 32

diversity of, 10
on forest floor, 27–28
importance of, 37–38
in understory layer, 23,
  24
see also trees
porcupines, 16

rainfall
  amount of, 7
  in canopy layer, 16, 18
  creation of, 10
  on forest floor, 27
  recycling and, 9–10
  in understory layer,
    23–24
rain forests
  area covered by, 4–6
  disappearance of, 32–34
  diversity of plants and
    animals in, 10, 32
  layers of, 12
  locations of, 5–6
ranching, 34
raptors, 15–16
recycling, 9–10
red fungi, 28
rosy periwinkles, 37–38
rubber, 37

seeds

About the Author

Stuart P. Levine has written several books on endangered animals and habitats. Holding degrees in wildlife education and psychology, he has worked with exotic animals for a number of years and has spent time in the rain forests of Nicaragua researching primate behavior. He currently works in Florida as a wildlife educator.